NATIONAL ANTHEM

NATIONAL ANTHEM

poems by

Kevin Prufer

Four Way Books
Tribeca / New York City

Distributed by
University Press of New England
Hanover and London

Editorial Office
Four Way Books
POB 535, Village Station
New York, NY 10014
www.fourwaybooks.com

Library of Congress Cataloging-in-Publication Data

Prufer, Kevin.
National Anthem : poems by / Kevin Prufer.
    p. cm.
ISBN-13: 978-1-884800-83-2 (pbk. : alk. paper)
ISBN-10: 1-884800-83-1 (pbk. : alk. paper)
I. Title.
PS3566.R814N38 2008
811'.54--dc22

                                    2007037694

This book is manufactured in the United States of America
and printed on acid-free paper.

Four Way Books is a not-for-profit literary press. We are grateful for the
assistance we receive from individual donors, public arts agencies,
and private foundations.

Distributed by University Press of New England
One Court Street, Lebanon, NH 03766

This publication is made possible with public funds from
the National Endowment for the Arts and from the
New York State Council on the Arts, a state agency.

NATIONAL
ENDOWMENT
FOR THE ARTS

State of the Arts

NYSCA

[clmp]
We are a proud member of the Council of Literary Magazines and Presses.

Contents

i

APOCALYPSE

Around that time, the city grew quiet.

You said Don't hurt me and I said If I was going to hurt you I'd have done it already.

We passed a dying store with gem-like windows. A door that banged in the wind. You said Let me go.

As in a film of the apocalypse, a breath of newspapers blew past us.

I won't hurt you, I said.

A car had expired in the street so I looked inside but there was nothing to eat.

The moon grew like an empire, then fell like a bomb

so I said it was an excellent night for a walk and we would find food in the dying city and take it back to share with the others, who were hungry.

Those days, the TVs stopped bothering us. The helicopters and the spotlights.

The city fell like the moon into an ocean, it was so sad and one night it rained and all the bodies in the graveyard washed away.

I'll tell you a story, I said, to make you stop crying for a minute. We walked down the darkening street.

I told you how the dead floated in their coffins like sailors, their boats unmoored and happy with the storm, all the way to sea.

The next morning, I searched the ground for rings and cufflinks, never finding any

and then I saw in a tree's low branch the body of a girl, long decayed. The flooding must have washed her there.

The sockets of her eyes were little caves for birds.

I touched her skull, then slid the gold ring from her dead finger. You laughed at that.

The city was a silence and the dead girl's ring felt tight around my finger. I won't hurt you, I said.

Beside a broken lamppost, you smiled. Such sharp teeth. We were always hungry then.

WE WANTED TO FIND AMERICA

We wanted to find America through the gasps of snow that fell like last century's angels—

And the starving horses, their shanks brittled over with ice—

And the moon atop its brilliant derrick, and the poor burning so beautifully in the oilfields.

As we drove, their cries lit the winds with wailing

and you said, *This isn't America* into the truck's dark cab and turned the radio loud.

Super 8, Waffle House, Motel 6, the half-lit parking lots off the exit where we pulled the truck and said we'd sleep

despite the gray-faced man unmoving by the payphone, despite the child asleep in the ice machine

and I closed my eyes so the theatre lights dimmed and my skull became a screen

and on it you were rich and happy, you were saying that you loved me.

And all night long, the nation reconstituted itself

so by dawn the light played its ringed fingers over the dashboard and said, *Wake up,*

fellow Americans, wake up and see what I have made for you,

Texaco, BP, Mobil and the road dusted over with jewels and snow. You were so cold

and beautiful, your hair undone, so we drove and drove. I said we'd see America—

the afternoon long as a bridal train, the horses falling in the oilfields.

As we pulled into Wichita the snow grew thick and clotted on the windshield, sleet falling like frozen pilots,

their legs shattering in the crowded streets. Hypodermic snow, pharmaceutical and sterile

and the office towers rose above us, their lights blinking like overstimulated cells and you said,

Darling, park the car, and you said, *Let's walk* and, *Look at the lights, how beautiful the lights are*

holding my hand in front of the Dillard's, the great chandelier that filled the room with shards,

that filled the street with blades, the chandelier like a perfect mind

and the office towers bending down to us as if they'd cup us in their hands and warm us,

as if they'd lift us from the street before we froze.

THE PASTOR

I was a long pew of lonely men.
                              The pastor said, *Kneel* and I kneeled.
The pastor said, *Rise* and, *Now we will sing.*

Outside, parachutes tangled in the trees. Soldiers unhooked their
harnesses and dropped to the ground while the parachutes gasped in
the sun like morning glories. The gunfire said, *Bang, bang, bang*

and the pastor said, *Kneel* and the old men kneeled. I kneeled.
The pastor said, *Bow your heads.*
                              The parachutes swayed in a wind
and from the woods the sounds of sticks cracking.

A morning glory expands like a man who has jumped from a plane.
Like a parachute.
                    The pastor lit a candle and another. The pastor
touched his chest here and here. The old men swayed in their shoes.

I was a pewful of such men,
                              eyes rolled back in my head. Weak and
trembly. How lovely the parachutes in the churchyard, their cords
twisting in the wind like a mission.
                              How lovely, the bells
that rocked on dowels in the tower, the sounds that slept in the hammer.
The hammer that swayed like a soldier beneath the bell.

The gunfire said, *Surprise,* said, *Ache.*
                              The pastor said, *Be seated!*
The pastor cleared his throat as though he had something to say,
holding his book before him.

In the churchyard a young man knelt by a tree.

Someone put a rifle in his mouth

and the pastor said, *Amen.*

The bell crashed through the tower.

A History of the American West

The American West slept on an open raft. His chest
was brown and flecked with hair. Hat tipped forward
to cover the eyes, one hand limp,

                                 cutting the water,
the other draped over the thigh, touching the thigh—
Skin like tobacco,

                  skin gone coarse and dry,
and like John Brown the sun rose and rose, then died
in the empty sky.

      ॐ

                      An eyelash twitched,
the eyeball rolled beneath the lid. Purse of lips,
the tongue that played behind the teeth in sleep.
The West

             was dreaming about fields, about a clutter
of rising birds, how they lift from the waving grass
like nets into the sky.

                    The raft turned in the current
and nudged the shore.

                    The West licked his drying lips,
dreamed now of a boy—himself—

      ॐ

                         on a horse,
looking over a field of singing birds,
off to the desert's edge, a clot of buildings, a shadow
on the sand around it.

                  From far away, the voices of girls
say, *Yes.* Say, *Come from the horse with your hat
and your leather.* Say, *How beautiful,*

                      your hair blown back

and filled with sand, cheeks red where the weather
bit them.
      The West smiled in sleep,
ran his tongue over sharpened teeth.

Years later, of course, our bombs destroyed the desert,
blooming like orchids.
              Years later, we watered the sand:
fallout, cancer, birds trapped in the cloud and down
to the dunes with them,
          the thud of breaking bodies,
wings torn back and rustling in the grass.
                One day
the sky was blue as an eye pinned open. Then the flash
and rush of wind, the stalk that rose and split,
and petals, gray and black.
          And lush.

In the dream, the girls say, *Lush.* Say, *Lips,*
wet where the dew has kissed them.
        And, *Sand*
caressing the hair blown back.
           Girls in the cluster
of a desert town,
      girls in the schoolyard
holding out their arms to him,
          and the West,
on his raft, dreams of ribbons, sunburnt legs, the West,
who has no family he remembers, the West,

raised on a raft or a plow,
                        who cannot recall,
but in the dream pushes westward on his horse,
into the sand.

        ❧

He slept and slept, stalled in the brush
                                at the river bank.
Water lapped against the raft. The smooth chest
rose and fell. Gorgeous in his jeans and sunburnt arms,
gone
        to the bomb blast and the gasp of time,
to Brigham Young and his wagonload of wives,
the heel and rein of men on horseback. The railroad,
the churn of every train.
                        Cather, Crane, and dustclouds
when, for weeks, the farms burned under rainless skies.

        ❧

The West content and tan, because that is his history,
caught in an eddy,
                        gone to everything but the gentle dream
in which the West rides westward, toward the desert town,
into the girls who crowd around,
                                who touch the horse's
sweat-damp coat, who stroke the shank, the saddle,
and his thigh—
                Lush. Lush, they say, then smile
and haul him down.

And the shopping center said, *Give me, give me.*

And the moon turning on its pole said, *I love you, you who have so much to give.*

And you said, *Darling, if you could just wait in the car for ten minutes and I'll be right out—*

And the sliding doors opened for you like a coat.

Then the car ticked like the contented in the catatonic snow

and the black boys at the bus stop laughed in their hoods until a bus dragged them through the night and away—

And a woman paced beneath the store.

Sometimes, I can hear the nation speak through the accumulation of the suburbs—

Olive Garden and Exxon; Bed, Bath & Beyond, the stars that throw their dimes around us all

until the eyes say, *Love* and the streets say, *Yes!* and the parking lot

fills with angels blowing past the lines of freezing cars.

You had been inside for longer than you said, and when you reemerged

I went to help you with the bags. *I'm sorry, sorry*—into the cold air—*I couldn't help*—

What was the body but a vessel, and what was the store but another, larger vessel? The keys sang in my numb fingers. The flag applauded in the wind.

And then I saw that you were smiling up at it.

THE EXCAVATION OF THE CHILDREN OF THE CZAR
They were posed, as if to have a portrait taken

We thought the shovels were a war above our heads.
Then voices and a spade
                        in my pockmarked shoulder bone
where a bullet lodged and pained the joints. Poor Ana said,
They've come to put us on display again,
                               and I laughed
and said it was a garden party.

And then a shaft of light to fill the skull holes.

They picked me up. My neck went slack.
                              Someone said
they'd take us to the lab and test what skin and hair remained.
And someone said, *A bullet* and *Another!* And Ana, who was wisest:
They'll prop us in a golden case. They'll drape a flag across our bones—

I've been a baby in a well. The air was damp. I cried and cried.
I've been a secret in another's brain, and then the brain went cold
so no one knew—
                     and now the jawbone aches to speak
or sing—

           Alexei, stop. The wind devoured the sails and Ana
leaned against the boardwalk's rail, holding her hat to her head
so the ribbons laughed in the storm.
                        A man tied up

his sailboat for the night; I climbed upon the rail to see.
Alexei, she said, *get down!*
                              I smiled and made a face.
Get down, she said, *you'll fall and hurt yourself.*
                                    I didn't care.

They packed us in a box and stowed us in a truck
and carried us away.

And then I fell
                    and, falling, cut my arm so Ana pulled me to her breast,
squeezed my arm to stop the blood, which never worked.
She took a ribbon from her hat and made a knot above the cut.
We hurried home through rain and up the palace steps,
where they put me in a room to heal,
                              where Ana scolded me.

The sun
bled through a crack in the back of the truck

And Ella said, *You shouldn't play so rough. I'll tell our father.*
She wiped a lock of hair from her wet forehead
                                        then kissed
my nose. She blew the candle out and closed the door.

When we arrived, a man unpacked our bones and spread them on a table.

The jawbone ached to speak, and the skull remembered:

They posed us in a room as if to take our picture.
Then the sound of gunfire from the camera.

Ancient Rome

When I found you
you were curled on a pew, asleep.

Someone had dressed you in rags and old columns.
Someone had covered you with yesterday's news.

And what was that for a pillow? A little cloth bag
of coins? Such eyes

like golden cups, such hair like silver tassels.
Why weren't you in the Forum

with the wreckage? The Coliseum
with the cameras and the thousand steps?

All over Rome, people were looking for you,
saddled with hip packs, trailing

their children. All over Rome,
with their thin wives and café tables.

As for me, I'd stepped in from the heat
and the vendors. The church was quiet

as a closed fist. What were you doing
beneath the mighty stained glass windows,

asleep like that
on your gold coins and hair?

The Fall of Rome

Comes like a hammer to a window, a thin crash.
Like a row of bees, angry, through the hole.
Or strange and unwanted, a pained guest,
a guest who has not long to live.

Come slowly, I tell it, and gentle as an evening.
Come unlike a bee sting—serene, harmless,
raining over the house, raining me asleep.
It would be good if it came in my old age like a blue wind

from a nest in the yard. If it came on quick wings by night,
while I slept on the couch, having finished for the day.
Or it would be good if it startled me and was over,
if all at once the sky went dark and the snow

was a cold sting I did not feel. If it came
like the frozen bee I found the other day,
no longer dangerous, but asleep. If it was like sleep,
curled on a rock in the snow. It is only a shell,

I wanted to say, its dead wings still against its husk.
It is only a wing that has stopped against the body, in the cold.
I can put so many names to it, none of them good.
It would be best if it had no wings at all.

The Minor Politician

They wrapped me in a cotton sheet
                    and pinned my eyelids closed,

then carried me down the mausoleum stairs
through halls that curved
                    like veins, then down again

and placed me on a shelf.

Because they did not know my ears were working still
they laughed and stole my rings.

And I had served my people well
                    (now dead and unimportant),
my thoughts of them like folded paper laws.

And I had served the senators
                    (the mice that gnawed my fingerstumps)
who said they loved me, wrapped me in a cloth.

Then years and years: bootstep of armies trudging overhead,
horse hoof, plow,
            a rumble I could never fathom—

When God reached from his cloud and, like a bomb,
he let a lightshaft through the ceiling

I loosed the rusted pins so I might see
                    his hand that groped the catacombs,
and touched the shelves that held the others' bones,

his hand that brushed the walls and found my corner

where he would take my body from the tatters
and lift me through the shadows
                              to the trees.

Landscape with Hospital and Empire

Then there is quiet.
              The hospital sleeps on the cliff.
Ice swath and storm—the sky gone bird-like, the leaves gone gray.
The fruit trees are griefless and still, creaking
                              like old knees in a stiff wind
and far below, where the cold sea licks the sand,
                         an ambulance idles.
How tiny, the driver seen from the hospital window. And chill.

This is the empire's edge. The blue sea salts the shore.
                           The Caesars,
cold in their beds, have paper skin and rings. They watch TV
or push the nurse-call buttons, eyes rolled white in their skulls.

And where can the slaves have gone? Over the blue and harrowing sea?
Where are the girls who play tambourines, who tap them
on their thighs and sing?
                     And where, the boy who juggles silver plates?
The three-armed man, the giant, the Nubian and his drums?

The gluey air is hot with breaths and glare.
                         The Caesars dream
of Rome. Gone, the snow. Gone, the stutter and the aged gait.
Away—in dreams—the hands that shook to take the scepter,
that dropped the plates
                and broke them on the floor.

They yearn to recreate
               the empire in gold and slaves.
The sun that filled the streets with glow, the Forum's shout.

A girl is selling favors from a booth, a tribune drinking wine
from a new clay bowl.

၆

The ambulance idles in the snow.
                              Ice has thrilled the windshield
with circuitry and cold. The driver smiles to see the hospital
teeter on the cliff
                and nearly fall.

The Caesars, he knows, are frail and old. The gods
have filled their skulls with snow
                              and time will throw the empire in the sea.

Ars Poetica

I've written love notes all my life—
the letter I dropped from the window, stained and yellow;

the one curled into the begger's cup.
The empire fell around me

like snow, so the citizens cringed in the streets,
their laces untied—blank-faced and strange.

I've written love notes and I do not know
to whom. In all directions, creased between bricks

or dropped from my fingers into gutters
so someone might find them and smile. Useless notes,

empty and vaguely
sad. I did nothing to help

while the empire limped into the park like a wounded car,
but composed while the crying shuddered

to a close and the buses stalled in the alleys.
Once, a group of hungry girls knotted on the street corner

called my name. Their hair was white
with snow, their lashes wet.

Love notes leaked from my hand as I walked past.
I have always been a gorgeous mind, light-in-the-eye

and dreaming. Always a work of art, a perfection
of limbs and hair, an arc in the marble

of my writing arm. Down and down my letters fell
while the empire closed.

What We Did With the Empire

We rolled it into the hide-a-bed, covered it in cushions, and left it near the curb for the students.

Then we buried it by the doghouse.

No! The well! I said, and you counted, *One, two, three,* until, from far away, the sound of a body striking water, beautiful really, like wind through wind chimes.

One time, you told me, *It will never fit*, waving the garbage bag like some kind of accusation. But I knew just the tool. It hung from a nail above the workbench.

So we tied a barbell to its ankles and threw it from a bridge—and down to the tour boats with it, where it sank among the ducks.

Sometimes it whispered in the night like a bad cold, rocking on its dismal heels beneath the hall light.

Sometimes it clattered through the house, dragging its chains as if it were a ghost.

When it spoke, it spoke a foreign language. Its gestures, too, I rarely understood.

You said, *It's too sad, too sad, really*, so we killed it again and shut it in the freezer and drove it to the dump.

It had such cold hands, playing over my ankles in the night. Breath, too, like tiny arctic blasts on my ears.

There is nothing so lonely as an empire detached from its people, you said, turning the page. The hour was time for bed.

It sat on the rocking chair, looking sincerely at the clock until I gave it the smile I call *mournful.*

I've been lonely, too. Uncared for and very sad. Sometimes the world just churns along, the people in the street passing like ghosts of themselves,

the tour boats on the river gone spectral in the moth light. Moon light. TV light.

It was late and I was hungry. I couldn't remember what I'd done with the knife.

DEAD SOLDIER

Where the living are, no one's missed him yet.
The best of them
                     will sing themselves to sleep.
The others laugh too loud and swallow pills
until their wet cells burst
                           beneath the skin like grapes
or bloom like urchins in a lukewarm sea.

    *

High above,
                the green moon glows in a windy sky
like a half-dead cat and its one good eye.

    *

And who will coin his eyes,
                      and who would care?
He who failed in school has failed again. And he
who slept last night in a narrow bed
                        will sleep in tents of sand
with the collapsing dead.

The boy who drowned in the bog, the boy caught in the rotors, the boy who laughed too loud—

The boy who swallowed the bee that stung the throat—

The ripcord worked, but the parachute fluttered weakly above and would not bloom—

He put his foot down in the foreign grass and heard a click, as of metal on metal. When he lifted that foot—

Sometimes it is a cold day and the clouds rain toxin over the boys on the base—

Sometimes, they don't know they're being watched, leaning against their packs, asleep like that—

One more, one more, he said. *One more all around*— And the assembled clapped for him, they clapped, he put his money down and smiled because they loved him—

Sometimes a boy thinks he is unloved, so he retires to a dark tent where he will not be disturbed—

Then, the cells wink out like lights on a tall office building in a strange city at dusk—

His friends said it was a sad day, it was very sad. They thought he'd been kidding, they told him not to laugh like that—

You pull the string and out it blooms—

And what was he doing off the base late at night? What was he doing on the open water, in the plane, driving so fast down unfamiliar roads? His mother—

Someone would tell her. Someone would write her a letter, thank God. There's a template for that—

A guy who puts your name on the hard drive, a distant office, a simple program and printer—

You punch in the name and out it comes.

THOSE WHO COULD NOT FLEE

The rain, like Caesar's army—
                And the city, aghast—
The old ladies huddled in the doorways,
                     obliterated
in the downpour, ladies like ghosts of themselves—
And you were saying,
              Why shouldn't we adopt?
A Chinese? A Romanian? A noble thing to do, these days,
and if the buildings burned
              we wouldn't see them
through the weather.

              Then the enemy
stealing through the thickets—blue faced and strange.
Our legions far outnumbered, the legions of Paulinus—
so who would save us?
             The aged and infirm who couldn't
leave the city?
          They'd string them up on posts,
they'd light the streets
             with slowly burning bodies.

How they hate us for our freedom, someone told me once,
How they loathe our freedom—
An old man tottered in the street;
                or the clubfoot
where his retreating family left him, huddled in his bed,
asleep—
        The killers in the thicket—

&

A child from far away, a Russian
                              or a black one.
You pulled your coat a little tighter
at the throat,
                    the thicket trilled with ghosts
assembled half of rain—and then of flesh.
                                        A bus
approached, not ours, and in my dented mind I swore
a black man dragged behind it—

&

                              They'd burn the city
and the ones who couldn't flee
they'd skin and nail to posts.

&

                              I only mean this
if we can't conceive. Our bus approached,
the crying of the brakes—
                          and some in their tattered
useless wings, and others curled in doorways,
their breath that filled the streets with fog—
How they hate our freedoms—
                          the doors and the pneumatic hiss—

᧞

Caesar's pointless extras and their ragged shields,
the white-faced files.

                     Those who had the legs to march
prepared to march away.

                     A good thing, you said, *a noble thing*—
a clatter of retreat, the pistons squeaked.

                            We had no choice.
We left the weak to perish in the street.

THE MOON IS BURNING

Such snow! I said. Then, *No,*
       smearing a bit of soot
between my fingers. *Not snow.* The moon crackled and glowed
above the trees. A single plume of flame
         like a petal
unfurled from a crater and disappeared

         in the night sky.
Orange moon, moon and the sparks that fell like cigarettes
or tiny empires to the ground.
        Ash in the hair and throat
so I ducked beneath the trees and wiped soot
from my eyes. My barn glowed on the hill
and the moon spun in its orbit,
        coughing smoke and flame.

I have often looked across the fields and the moon said,
You have only a short time, your kind. I paid it no mind.
Everything is always
      talking. Dark moon, crescent, half, afire,
moon that skimmed the distant mountains
beyond which the Capitol slept,

moon that reddened them—and cast the city, I guessed,
in a lovely glow.

I offered these to the Republic: my ashy coat the moon ruined.
My shoes which after a time were thick with soot.

                                                    A horse.
They wouldn't do. And soon

                                        the houses came awake and spilled
their lights over the blanketed landscape. My neighbors
shielded their eyes to watch
                                        the moon that wobbled in the sky,
that hissed and spit and fell. They groaned

and coughed into their hands, then turned the radios on
to static.
            They stayed all night and watched it shed itself
and shrink—nickel, flame, then pinprick. Then they went to sleep.

Here in the provinces, news comes slowly.
                                        We are a simple people,
and live as if concealed. The next morning, we shoveled ash away
and went about our business. A roof or two had caved.

I waited for your letter from the city,
                                        but it never came.

34

Who Are Our Barbarians?
—Suburbia

Lock the door. Press the red button
so the alarm goes on.

Perhaps you have seen one disappear
over the wall. Perhaps a scrap

of shirt on the barbed wire. Footprint
where the rosebush grows.

Maybe you would touch one like a fetish.
Oiled and smooth. Warm,

then cooler. Cold. A knife might take
the heart out. A pear in the hand, sopping

like yours. Knife to the belly
where the last meal sleeps. What

does it tell you?
They are always dying. Every day,

the fingers curl into buds.
A wailing from the park that woke us all.

Heavy lidded like tired dolls.
When they recline, the eyes snap shut.

THE WAR DEAD

Slap of sea against the old hull, the tip and fall of footsoles on the gangplank
as the dead descend—

        the ship gone quiet, asleep at the dock.
The dead drift down the gangplank

          to the steaming shore
where no one meets them—

        I am always dreaming about those
who left their bodies halved in fields I'll never see—

(The brain in the bomb case that guides the thrusters—
The camera that is its silvered eye—

         Its scales flash in the sun
as it passes.)

For them, I have walked the lonely aisles of shipyards after dark
dreaming of oil wells.

       For them, I have stood among the ropes
and looked to distant islands—

        I have dials in my brain, like a bomb—
I have an eye that records—

At times, I'd build myself a ship

        to sail to them—
The dead, who have everything to tell me—

         The bombs that disjoint
their fallen bodies—

So they might gather at the shore to watch my ship,

                         almost material—

So the light might filter through them—

So they might tell me where we're going, the sad boys,
one moment, awake, then canceled—

                    the boys who never saw
the bombs that broke them,

no one to burn them in their armor

                or build a heap of stones.

THE AFTERLIFE

Here are boys, still weak. When they speak
                              snow falls from their lips.
Pale of hand and cheek, the motors that whirred in their chests
have failed.

    ❧

Their new city—buildings like a scrim
                              a god unfurled for them
so it waves in the wind.

    ❧

Pallid, strange, and chill.
The boys are laughing weakly in the street

    ❧

so the snowbanks build and stir.
                              It is a city of lost children,
of failures: the weakhearted, pigeon-toed, transparent lispers,
the recently dead who have no name for it,
                              or do not care

    ❧

to name it. An empty time they had, coming here—
                              a long ride
on a quiet train, and now, on the moonlit avenue,
they talk among themselves.
                    A boredom, one says, over the rails.
Someone nods. *I was thinking of the good things, candy,*
when at last the coughing stopped.

ॐ

For my part—I have grown
                    accustomed.
My window that overlooks more buildings and the bay,
                                    the voices
and the endless snow. Like anyone, of course,

ॐ

I expected a better landscape—a warmer breeze,
                                    a breath, a relaxation
of the senses. *Canceled, canceled.* A passage like moving
from one town to another, warmer town,
                                    but the city is new,
the population pale, unsteady. *When at last they covered me up—*
the coughing stopped.
                    I counted on a god and, thus,

ॐ

judgment—a smile from above, a *You have passed* or not. A hand
from the clouds to lift me up,
                                    a gentle voice to call me
blameless.
            The boys in the street below
search for their wallets. The city squats on the bay, and I,
who am one of them,
                    smile at the squalls from their mouths

৵

as, from far away, another train pulls into the station,
sighs, and, with a shudder,

                                   stops.

ii

History

They put a bottle in my neck
and threw me from the bridge into the river
where I floated on my back then sank.

I slept for weeks beneath a log, then
woke to the light flittering through cold water.

Chilled over, thick in the tongue and sweet—
I could not speak, so watched instead
the bits of silt that fell like dead embers

over my eyes.

GIRLS IN HEAVEN

Sometimes, it rains for days
so we crawl into our cabin beds.
       My eyes snap shut
like a doll's. The pink spot on the cheek, a plastic flush
that stains the neck, queer thrill of lace
           where the throat begins—
I am always dreaming

of satellites
winking over the seascape like sewing needles,

of a boy's hands
that crack the seam of the bluest egg.

Or it is a windy day so the houses quake on their stilts,
the palm trees waving their arms at the sea.

How did you happen to—the blond girl says.
I felt a little faint, collapsed
       in the pool of my skirt.
Where were you?
     The rowboat made me dizzy and I fell.
Silence.

I had a palpitation,
     a bird in my throat that wouldn't sing.
My father far away hunting deer and I, standing in the rowboat,
a parasol, ache, a boy's voice, singing
       and the sound of oars.

44

～

More dreaming—a boy's hands on his oar,
                              the smile
of cut water, laughter. When I open my mouth, birdsong—

～

Days pass, then sun.
                    We lie on our backs on the dock.
A fluttering of pages in the breeze. No, hair. Waves.
Do you remember?
                    The brain retards and, yes—it was sun-drenched
the day I died, my head grown hot, my fingers—
                                        an ache
in the thigh, so deep—

～

The girls talk among themselves,
nodding like flowers in a breeze. *So perfect here,*
so fine, nothing to worry—
                          the wind unknitting the voices,
a blinking—satellite, eye—above them—

～

and one morning another ship stopped in the harbor,
the low groan of embarkation.
                          The ramp fell like an arm.
A chuff of sails, foremast creak, and girls
drifting down the low slope
                          to the crowded shore.

Then the scalpel cuts the chest so the eyes roll back.
                                        Blood from the mouth,
from the bit tongue, and the face
                                tear-streaked and red. The other hand
fisted at the platform's edge. The restrained body
                                        speaks.

     ℘

It is snowing outside, snow
                        like little tranquilizers all over the yard,
snow like baby teeth, but so many of them! *Such weather,*
a teacher on the playground says, sweeping her hands so the boys look at it.
I have never seen
                such weather! Snow on the swings, over the jungle gym,
covering the woodchips. Listen—

     ℘

The body on the platform says, *I don't know. I don't know, I don't know.*

It closes its eyes. An incision, and another.
                                        Beneath the canvas straps
it sighs and shakes its head while snow gathers on the windowsill,
sweeps against the glass,
                        the glass decorated over with a maze
of lies. No, lace. Ice. The body wants to rise, but can't

     ℘

and, outside, the boys on the playground want to roll in the snow,
to throw the snow into the air so it falls over them,
                                        whitens their hair.

The teachers laugh because, *November and here it comes already,*
down and down, an insulated hush.

ॐ

The doctor says, *Observe,* and the incision smiles, openmouthed. *Clamp,*
clamp, holding out his hand. *Sponge,*
                                        slopping water over the chest
to wipe it clean. The eyes roll back and back,
                                        into the skull's white weather,
the patient gone and dreaming now, the patient in another time,
                                                        outside,
playing in the snow—

ॐ

                    He is playing in the snow,
                                        among boys
who push him down and bury him—

THE ENORMOUS PARACHUTE

The parachute fell over the suburb,
draping the houses with nylon and rope.
And where were you?
                              Far away and half asleep—

❧

A letter: Dear X—
                              The nylon is so lovely on a warm fall night
when the breezes fill it. In the porch light's glow, it takes on that gentle blush
of your cheek and I want to rise and touch it
                                                  or wrap myself in it.
The birds make scratching sounds where the cords have caught their legs.
Otherwise, it's very quiet here and I miss the stars.
                              And you, love, K.

❧

On the third night, I walked from my house
                              to find that place where the nylon
ended. I followed a single cord stretched down the street
and over a rooftop.
                              In some regions, the parachute draped so low
I had to duck or hold the nylon up with my fingertips.
                                                  Elsewhere,
it wagged high above me, suspended from gables or treetops.

Always, I thought of you asleep on the sofa in your robe, the TV on,
the quiet house
                              beyond the parachute.

❧

I camped beside an empty swimming pool
                              and watched the parachute shimmer
over the street lamps.

❧

Days, the sun filled it, spreading the light evenly
over the neighborhood.
                    In time, I became accustomed to that—
the parachute glowing pink each morning, then white-hot by afternoon.

❧

Dear X—
          Remember how I first kissed you in the parking lot, the hush
that fell over us when at last I released you? The parachute is like that,
but lasts longer.
          A dog approached me warily today, growled, then,
when I held out my hand, licked it. He accompanies me now.
                                        We eat scraps
from the refrigerators of those who fled in time, and we sleep, sometimes,
in their beds. Love—

❧

Frost came early, then sleet
                    drumming its fingers on the fabric.
Where the parachute tore, icicles formed, hanging dangerously
over the streets.
                    Some were enormous and lovely, cascading along
the parachute's gullies and runnels. Others more delicate, hundreds

lining the seams.

                  When the temperature rose the next morning
I heard them crash into the streets.

∾

Early winter light from holes torn in the fabric

                                      like long fingers.
I followed the cord, but could not find the end.

∾

Dear X—

            Sometimes I despair of ever discovering the parachute's edge,
or returning to you.

It sags and heaves in the wind. When there's rain, I drink from the runoff
that spouts from the holes.

                          Were you here, I'd show you that place
where I climbed through a hole and saw the parachute stretched for miles,
dune-like, snow-like, tenting over the trees and houses. So beautiful,
I know you'd agree,

               and terrible.

Migrating birds, unable to find sustenance or a branch to rest on,
die over the parachute.

At night I dream of you, sunlight, sometimes the shore.

                                     Yours, K.

And then, one winter day, I found not the edge of the parachute
but that place where the cords came together at its center,
                                        the length
I'd followed lifting suddenly into the air where it tangled in the high trees,
with a starburst of others.
                        The dog panted beside me, then barked,
and far above our heads, suspended from a harness,
                                        a dead man swung.

Dear X—
        We buried the man at that point below the center of the parachute
and made of his rucksack a crude memorial.
                                I did not have any books,
so recited a bit from a hymnal I found moldering on a church floor. Then,
unsatisfied, I read to him from this account.
                                You have, no doubt,
moved on by now. For my part—I will rest here
in the shelter of the parachute and the steeple's shadow
                                        until spring—

GOTHIC: LEAVES

The leaves fell out of the trees
and feathered the grass.
        The birds dropped, too, all morning,
their way-too-human eyes rolled back, then black
and gone—
        So, stripped and, for once, visible,
the naked twigs—
        hob-fingered, tack-fingered.
My mother in her rocking chair: *Best clean that up.*

Don't drive through piles of leaves, she said,
children play there.
        She rocked in her chair. *Crick, crick.*
Heaps of leaves on the roadside—boys
buried in them, leaves in their brittle hair,
        stopping their mouths
so they couldn't speak—

        Leaf rot and bristle—
The mounds of leaves and the bodies inside,
the wind grown chill and mean. *Soon*, she said,
it'll be winter.
        Best bring that dead wood in.
The naked branches tapped the windowpanes,
but never broke them.

WHO ARE OUR BARBARIANS?
—The museum

How we love them
when they are singing and simple

in gorgeous sneakers.
Invite them in, touch their eyes

until they sprout. Touch their mouths
with art. Hush, hush—

Soon they will speak. Then a tour,
so the slack mouths unfurl

and those many colored
birds fly out!

Or: call them from their hovels.
Then, in their blister lips, in their shackles

and downcast looks, their nervous rows,
you can paint them, quick,

with brushes and gouache.
Mount them

on the wall. Our barbarians
are fleet to the touch and,

like paintings, lovely.

CARAVAGGIO'S BENT NARCISSUS

And then I went down to the shore
                              to watch the ship fail in the shallows.
It tilted in the sun on a rotting keel, the topmost planks
gone white in the salt breeze,
                              the foremast split where the wind
undid it, billage swamped and rotting

where my friend the boatswain floated with his gear.
I have been these years

a friend only to the birds and things that burrow in the sand—
frigate dove, spermcrab,
                    a kind of cormorant I'd never seen before,
and so named bloodbird for the shock of red across its skull.
The boatswain—

                    he spun in the brine in the ship's full belly
where he dove one day to fetch a length of rope
                                        and caught his foot,
so could not re-emerge. I missed him so—
my friend, whose skin grew loose around his bones.
                                        Each night

჻

came rains and wind, so every dawn less ship remained.
Soon, I knew, I'd be alone no longer—
                                        a stormsurge
would rock the keel from its wedge of sand, would dash it on the stones,
and thusly break the boatswain free

჻

                                    so he might drift toward shore,
limbs slack in the storm-tossed sea, red hair fanned like lotus weed
around the sleeping face,
                        and eyes that never twitch beneath doll lids—

჻

his gentle body floating to an inlet where it could sink—

჻

                                        where, one day,
like Caravaggio's bent Narcissus, kneeling down to rinse my hands,
I'd spy his strange, attenuated face
                                peering up through silent water,
so I might bring it to my own to drink.

For My Father

When I'd achieved a certain distance from the shore,
                                          the gulls, also,
abandoned me,
              so I only heard the waveslap on the coffin's keel,
the uneasy grind of oars against the wooden rim—

    ∽

                                          In the distance,
what I took for islands: cloudbanks, soot-black in the salty air—
                                                    I hove
the coffin's sail and stowed it with my things.
                              The clouds bore up

    ∽

until I was a beaten dog, my coffin turning in the sea's eye—
Where had my father gone?
                        Black squall, windlash,
rain to turn the bones to glass and shatter them,

    ∽

my father, far away as the storm bore down.
                                    I lay on the planking,
the oar against my chest, looked up to the rainblast
                                          until my eyes closed

    ∽

and, at last, sleep took me—
                        and such dreams, then: the stormclouds
parting on an island; the coffin, its unearthly
                              speed into the cove

&

where I dragged it to the sands and looked about:

mist and, again,

the call of gulls. It was, as I'd imagined,

the very island

the dead inhabit,

&

and from the mists my father's transparent form—
such paleness in it, as I'd imagined.
When I pulled him to me, my arms passed coolly through
what at first I took for flesh—

he could not speak; I'd heard they couldn't—
but smiled and shook his head

and from his mouth the sound that gulls make.

&

It is the sadness of my life—

the coffin churning on the waves,

the storm long guttered past and turning in the distance, my father
diaphanous—

I'd have given him my blood to drink—

Mechanical Bird

Hard to cut the heart from the ribcage.
                              The skinflap opens
as a door opens to a darker room. Tease it with a finger,
                                        scalpel and clamp—
then coax it out and put it on a platter.
                              Hard to cut the heart, or replace it,

though a mechanical bird suffices nicely,
                              nested in the chest's
warm cavity. Intricate and Victorian, neatly feathered,
                                        yellow, wound tight
so it sings and turns its geared head, so the wings spread
                                        and flap. Sparrow,
chickadee, songbox that thrills and pumps the blood.

Don't you know this is a love poem?
Don't you know this is a poem about longing?
                              Lovely, the bird in the chest
that sings these words to it,
                    that beats its wings against the ribs' restraints.

Kneeling Man: Paused Footage

When time stops, the bullet hangs in the air,
                              a vapor trail behind it.

The target kneels on the sidewalk.
                    From his mouth,

the low sound of bells,
then nothing. Rain.
                    An open mouth and nothing from it.

It's always raining in this picture, the drops suspended in the air
like little glass dolls' eyes,

the bullet suspended like a larger eye in the middle of the frame.

Were the film to resume, the man might crumble into pavement.
The man might fall backward, sideways,

might teeter for a moment on his knees as if startled,
touch his chest gently,
                    then look at his hands.

⁊

From his mouth the bells continue, the bullet gliding like an innocent

⁊

to the other side of the frame.

A Severed Cow's Head

I wanted, almost, to touch the single eye
                                        that failed
to roll back to the skull's dim heaven. Pinpricked
pupil, eyewhite matte and shot
                                with red—the eye
that hadn't had enough

∾

                        of the world: scrub field
the cut head pressed against, and rain that died
on the mud-splattered face, the melting snow—
I could not help

∾

                        but recall that friend who, at 22, suddenly
knew he was dying. He cried outside
his neighbor's door, knocked,
                                until she called the police,
until he fell from the porch
                        into her garden,
where, hours later, an officer found him.
I cannot say if his eye—

∾

                        The cow kept watching
as rain undid
                the swiftly melting, snowy field,
as the sun rolled down the barn's black roof
into blacker trees.
                        Some of the hairs in its muzzle

were white, others moth-wing gray.
I won't know how to say goodbye when,

                                       at last,

I have to.

The Party by the Lake

Such a time we had at the lake those days—Janie with her catamaran
calling to the shore
                and Wilson, who was always game,
tipping his gimlet back, laughing with the others
who smoked their cigarettes
                   and died all morning.

Such a blear and thrill,
                  the sun that trilled the windowsill with cobwebs,
the sun that lit the lake and made of its surface a shiny pan—

Times like those I was a kind of angel,
my silver wings dragging in the dirt behind me,
                        my ragshop hair
that glowed like the light before a storm—

The lord had given me a voice that made the others swoon and sing,
that made them sigh—*Oh, sing!* and *sing!* from Janie,
                  and, *Yes, old boy*, from the men—
I was an empty vessel, a box of sound.

Then the black night fell around us like a wing—
Janie tying up the boat, and Wilson done and staggering,
his chair atilt
         then fallen on the dock,

and I gone, too, in the head, one drink too many,
wet of lip and strange,
           thin-wristed in the cold night air.

❧

I dragged my wings across the planks
and stood in my feathers and golden hair
to look to the distant town,

                           a row of crumbled teeth.

The moon fell like a match over the corpse of the party.

When I opened my mouth to sing

                            a rasp came out—
no, nothing, nothing—as the stars untied their strings
and on the lord's command

                        they fell.

THERE IS NO AUDIENCE FOR POETRY

They wanted him to stop kicking like that—
it made their eyes corkscrew, drilled the sun in the sky
so light dumped out like blood from a leak.
The boy in the trunk wouldn't die.

They drove and drove, and he dented the trunk's tight lid,
called their names, then pounded the wheel wells
with a tire iron. The sun filled
their skulls so they felt like hell

and the boy in the trunk wouldn't listen. You'd think
it was burning hot in there, you'd think he'd be gone,
passive, but no. The boy in the trunk
banged on and on

until the noise grew godalmighty unforgivable
and they had no choice but to pull into the woods,
leave the car, try to hitch a ride with someone
quieter, someone who could

listen without interrupting. They'd had a hot day.
The road simmered to the overheated sky.
But from far away they still heard him, the boy
in the trunk, his empty cry.

PRAYER

You'll find me in a suitcase. You'll find me in a car.
Lord, unbend my legs. Lord, lift me so I see.
The red moon in winter is the memory of candles,
the sky like church windows the sun nods through.
Lord, you'll find me in a dead car. I'll be gone in the trunk,
birds around my head and a mouthful of glass.
Birds that spin the head, Lord, and blood on my chin.
Am I ugly like this, hands roped at the back? My eyes
closed tight? Touch my face with your palm,
with your rough old hands that worked too hard—
A car in the field where the weeds grow high,
the trunk closed tight so no air gets in. Unknot me,
lift me to a glassy sky. Your lovely mallet arms—
I can't describe the arms that you must have.

Apple Trees and Street

The little death in the apple's core says, *Darling*,
says, *Sweetheart*, all wrapped around its juice.
A slick breeze sways the tree, unpastes the leaves.
Oh, ticket the pick-up windshields with apple leaves,
kiss the boys in the trucks with chlorophyll and veins.

The world is falling falling like gluey twigs.
The bees devour the flowers or sting them
into rot while high on a branch, the little death
in the apple's core says, *Sweet*, says, *Touch me
and I'll fall*. All around, thin boys in trucks

idle at stop lights or look blankly toward the trees.
Cover their trucks with leaves and falling apples,
splatter them with rot and seed and flesh.
The boys grow sleepy. Their engines growl—
while the death in every apple explodes its core.

PLAYGROUND

It's easy to forget they're mortal—
                                  the boy climbing
the slide's tall ladder—

          ❧

the child beneath the swing set, crying for his mother,
face like a petal—

          ❧

                     and the clouds spill water over them so they'll grow,
and the mothers on the long park benches talk among themselves,
heads swaying on stems—

          ❧

                        they are only memories now,
they are dying weeds. Autumn, and the leaves coughed and died in the trees.
Sometimes

          ❧

                I imagine a kind of grace was given me. I am small again,
thin-wristed and amnesic,

          ❧

                        and God, who lives in the high leaves, God,
whose head is crowned in twigs, whose many-jointed fingers
                                        scrape down
through seed pods—

&

Like everything, leaves die on the branches

&

and the child cries on the playground. He'll cry
                                        until he disappears.

A Boy Like Your Mother

Once I was flush so I drank until the walls grew vague.
A guy at the bar said, *Who's the boy?*
                              and I touched your hair
and bought you another Coke while evening dropped over St. Louis
like a bird to its nest.
                    Last call, the call girl said. *Drink up.*

❧

So I found the car.
                    I thought we'd know America better, you and I,
and we drove the highways outside of the city.

When it rained the drops were hypodermics on my arm
and the night went on
                    like a handful of pills thrown against the sky.

❧

I thought you'd get to know me, but you cried
                              then, finally, slept—

❧

Who could talk to a boy like that, so stainless and asleep,
your mother home and cursing all night long—
                              Missouri and the boxcars
rattling past like strings of coffins,
                    and you beneath the radio's green light,
curled on the seat—I thought I knew you—

&

You'll miss me when I'm dead,
your old dad who took you out and bought you shoes,
the radio gone to country,
                                    then to static,
and your even little breaths, mechanical and strange.

&

I was afraid to touch you,
                                afraid to wake you up,
as dawn cast the silos into distant silhouettes
and made them look like giants
                                    stalking through the fields.

CICADA SHELL

It is a shell, if by shell I mean something emptied,
crawled out of.

I hate the beetle grip on the screen door, the abdomen
like an extinguished bulb.

In its translucence, the possibility of ocean

or crackle, were it to fall driftingly to the porch floor
and be stepped on—

Someone should fill it with light.
Give me a syringe. I will inject it

with maple syrup. A cicada shell should be
amber to the tongue,

a little death in every husk

so the yard is full of mourning.
The trees, on their leaves, shudder—a warp and wail of legs,

a click in the bug-larynx.
I'd swallow them like pills if they contained

their own rejuvenation. I'd let them wobble
like drugs in my palm.

My father died last night. I was far away.

I want to pop them like grapes between my fingers.
Their juice is sweet in my useless hands.

LEUKOTOMY

They carved a cave in my head,
                           then slid a knife blade in
so all I saw was cloudburst. My fingers twitched and ached,
then wouldn't move at all.
                        No one said the rains would fall
like needles dropped in handfuls from the clouds.
The knuckle at my temple made the sound of wind, a liquid
trickling from my hairline
                      back behind the ear. The doctor
moved his fist, the knife cut through the nerve's stiff fingers,
and so I was asleep.

∿

                    Such dead weather
untethered neurons make, a rattling as of rainlash
at my windows, a struggle—brutish wind against my door.
I slept on the table—I knew I slept—
                        and in my skull's
dull bowl it poured and poured until my head felt soppy wet
and churning from the storm.
                    And from far away I heard
applause, *Well done, young man,* a pause.
You have the fingers of an artist. Such skill.
The rain
        that dampened my windowsill,

∿

the rain that drummed my eyelids white, then gathered in the holes
that were my ears and chilled them there.
                    The rain gone colder now
and sleet-like, snowy as the coats of surgeons, white

like streetlamps through the haze of snow. *Well done, well done.*
He'll sleep another hour.

> *A calmness has befallen him.*

❧

And with it, a memory of winter—

> A child snug in a cave

he made in the snowplow's pile, fingers numb and worthless,
mittened over.

> I'd smoothed the walls and patted down the dome.

I'd cut a window in the snow and called my father

> who never heard.

Look—I waved—*look.* He kicked the snowplow into gear
and lit a cigarette. *Look*, and then a shifting from the walls.
The ceiling glowed and moved. I turned around,

> and down

the snow fort fell. My eyes were full of it, my mouth. I coughed,
but couldn't move. My arms went needled over,

> numb—

❧

the skull collapses just like that, the eyes black

> and pointless.

The surgeons in the hall, white coats hanging—
they smile, then pat the youngest on the back.
Good work, they laugh, *good work.* The skull:
there'd always been a hole in it.

> My nerves had frozen there.

The Mean Boys

The mean boys beneath the Exxon light off Route 64
had quick eyes
and pockets full of dollar bills, like secrets they'd stolen.

Their pickups on idle, radios going, hands pale in the glare
like moths—at their lips,
at their snowy hair, touching the pickups' fenders. Mean and thin,

laughter too loud for a Sunday night, for the snow
like flecks of sad gray paint
peeling down over Lockwood and the town at its televisions.

The moon was a bright wreckage that fell over the rock quarry
where the mean boys' fathers
worked. Fell over the roofs of trailers, over the frozen

river, where no one saw it come down. The mean boys didn't care.
Their feet were strewn
with broken glass, arms bruised at the shoulders, cigarettes

curled into their sleeves. This was long ago. I pass here some nights
but the lot is always empty.
The snow has painted the town away, and I miss the flash

when they opened their mouths to laugh.

Improper Elegy

The circuitry of frost on the kitchen window
and the thought that hums inside it—

A cold night, a dead night.
Snowfall's shower of data in the yard—

the freezing deathflowers, pasteflowers,
the blooms that nod and sleep on their stems

until each petal dies gratefully into the windowbox—
I don't know what to do

with the doomed, the chilled over and gone,
but drink until my fingers become twigs

and, like twigs, snap.

Someone cut a hole in my head and poured a poison in,
so the kitchen becomes

the sum of all its information: The onion,
asleep in its paper skin, the wine, the knives

that smile in the drawer. The refrigerator hums
and loves the winter weather, the snow

and flowers that make a deathbed of it,
woolflowers, hatflowers, the dying fisted rose.

A pulse of information.

ॐ

A drink would be perfect right now,
and another, to take me out the back door

and into the snow
where I'd stand in my slippers and watch

pills fall from the sky. The cold air undoes
the throat and makes me blink. A wind coughs

in the trees. What have I done with my time?
You have been dead a year now

so I hardly think about you anymore.
Look—the houselights are glowing.

They glow like angry little screens.

Elegy: Airport

Then there was snow
                     on the plane's dead wing,
over the hull that stretched like a seedpod,
killing the windshield,
                     clogging the flaps,
dying and dying in the pall of night.

Then it occurred to me: *petal-like,*
like petals detached and adrift on a breeze
or down from a vase-full,
                     where they'd wilt and curl,
the blossoms that nodded
                     on a curving stem.

It is, perhaps, better,
                     is mercy and numb—
but I couldn't believe it.
The airport was still and the snow just died
on the corpselike planes
                     in their vanishing rows.

DYING BIRD

The ground kept rising toward it—
A bloom in the garden plot, a tangle

of stem-thrust and flowerbed.
The bird sputtered over the roof tiles,

died over them—
then fell into the chimney's throat,

into the house, where I, a boy, was reading.
It lay on the hearth, a soft mound.

Later, I would think about it,
and look out the window

into the snow. I read how one winter
soldiers posed the Czar's children in a parlor

far from home, as if for a photograph,
then shot them. They left a trill on the wall.

My brother cried at dinner when he learned
one day he would die. I picked at my food

and wanted to be a chip in the wall
or a spot that would not wash away.

My mother took him to his room.
The bird lay on the hearth

and wouldn't move. Its wings traced
an arc in the soot. I watched

for a long time, but never touched it.

Acknowledgments

American Poetry Review: "National Anthem"

Black Warrior Review: "The War Dead"

Boulevard: "Improper Elegy," "The Excavation of the Children of the Czar," "Girls in Heaven," "We Wanted to Find America," "Landscape with Hospital and Empire," "Those Who Could Not Flee"

Cincinnati Review: "Kneeling Man: Paused Footage"

Colorado Review: "There Is No Audience for Poetry," "Army Tales"

Conduit: "The Party by the Lake"

Court Green: "Apple Trees and Street"

Epoch: "What We Did with the Empire"

Field: "Prayer," "Gothic: Leaves," "The Pastor," "Mechanical Bird"

Laurel Review: "The Minor Politician"

Lyric: "A History of the American West," "For My Father"

Margie: "Ars Poetica"

Mid-American Review: "Dying Bird," "The Enormous Parachute"

Natural Bridge: "Ancient Rome"

New England Review: "Leukotomy," "Playground"

The New Republic: "Dead Soldier," "Airport: Elegy"

Ploughshares: "Apocalypse," "The Afterlife"

Prairie Schooner: "Caravaggio's Bent Narcissus," "Who Are our Barbarians," "Who Are our Barbarians"

Shade: "The Fall of Rome"

Shampoo: "The Mean Boys"

Swink: "The Moon Is Burning"

Verse: "Cicada Shell"

Verse Press: "Ars Poetica"

Virginia Quarterly Review: "A Boy Like Your Mother," "Surgical Theatre"

"A History of the American West" was reprinted in the 2007 *Pushcart Prize* anthology.

Many of these poems also received the 2004 and 2006 George Bogin Award of the Poetry Society of America and the 2005 Stanley Hanks Memorial Award.

"What We Did with the Empire" is for Craig Morgan Teicher, whose work inspired it. "We Wanted to Find America" is inspired by a poem by Alvin Greenberg.

"Dead Soldier" also appeared as a limited edition broadside, designed by Amber McMillan, and printed by the Center for Book Arts in New York City.

Thanks to the National Endowment for the Arts for financial support and to the University of Central Missouri for encouragement and time to write. Thanks to Mary Hallab, Sally Ball, Joy Katz, R. M. Kinder, Alan Michael Parker, Eric Miles Williamson, and Wayne Miller, all of whom read and offered criticism about many of these poems.

This book is for my father.

Kevin Prufer is the author of *Fallen from a Chariot* (Carnegie Mellon, 2005) and *The Finger Bone* (Carnegie Mellon, 2002), among others. With Wayne Miller, he's also editor of *New European Poets* (Graywolf, 2008) and *Pleiades: A Journal of New Writing*. He is the recipient of three Pushcart prizes and a 2007 fellowship from the National Endowment for the Arts, and his poems have appeared in *Best American Poetry, Boston Review, The New Republic, Virginia Quarterly Review,* and elsewhere.